Now We're Getting Somewhere

The Felix Pollak Prize in Poetry

The University of Wisconsin Press Poetry Series
Ronald Wallace, General Editor

Now We're Getting Somewhere • David Clewell

Henry Taylor, Judge, 1994

Now We're Getting Somewhere

David Clewell

The University of Wisconsin Press

The University of Wisconsin Press
114 North Murray Street
Madison, Wisconsin 53715

3 Henrietta Street
London WC2E 8LU, England

5   4   3   2   1

Printed in the United States of America

Library of Congress Cataloging-in-Publication Data
Clewell, David, 1955–
    Now we're getting somewhere / David Clewell.
    96 p.   cm. — (The Felix Pollak prize in poetry)
    ISBN 0-299-14410-0   ISBN 0-299-14414-3 (pbk.)
    I. Title. II. Series.
PS3553.L42N68   1994
811'.54 — dc20   94-10665

for Patricia, co-conspirator in these matters:
all my crackpot love

Contents

III. Lost in the Fire

IV. In the Boondocks of What's Possible

Acknowledgments

Grateful acknowledgment is made to the editors of the following publications where these poems first appeared:

ABRAXAS: Why Certain Poets Have No Business at the Track
BOULEVARD: If the Wisdom Holds
THE CHARITON REVIEW: The Final Meeting of the Pessimists Club
DOUBLE TAKE: A Long Way from the Starlight
THE GEORGIA REVIEW: What Some People Won't Do   .
HARPER'S: In Case of Rapture
THE KENYON REVIEW: Lost in the Fire
THE MISSOURI REVIEW: Goodbye Note to Debbie Fuller: Pass It On; In
          Case of Rapture; Lessons in Another Language
NEW ENGLAND REVIEW: Do Not Disturb
ONTARIO REVIEW: Carnival Heaven
PIVOT: The Anatomy of Wishful Thinking; But Seriously
POETRY: America's Bed-and-Breakfasts; From the Other Side, Houdini Tries
          to Come Through for Bess; I Can't Believe the Face on Mars
RIVER STYX: Holding On
SHENANDOAH: She Dreamed She Was Writing a Love Poem
YANKEE: Vegetarian Physics

"Lost in the Fire" appeared in a limited edition chapbook from Garlic Press (St. Louis). Special thanks to Pete "G-Man" Genovese.

A few of these poems appeared in *This Particular Eden* (Southwest Missouri State University, 1992), an anthology presentation of Missouri Biennial Writing Award winners. My gratitude to the Missouri Arts Council for its generous support.

I. Fresh Out of Dreams

On nearly every radio at night there is some off-the-wall talk show to be found, with zany chatter and beyond-the-fringe commentary. The kind of talk one never finds by day. Callers' voices become slurred after 3 AM, their contentions more baroque.

—John Bowers, *In the Land of Nyx*

If the Wisdom Holds

The first time I woke up as a kid
screaming out of a dream, I really thought
it was all over, the little I knew of my life.
Yet there I was, a small but undeniable fact
sweating out another troubled night in my own bed.
How was I to know the conventional dreamland wisdom:
people never quite seem to die in their own dreams.
They always catch themselves right before hitting
bottom, right before the bullet slams home.
And out of nowhere they're awake,
not dead in the least, although they may discover
themselves buried deep in pillows, even sheets
pulled over their heads. The panicky breathing
is one sure sign, the undertaker's own bad dream.
Or else in that last split-second of REM theatrics
there's a desperate change of scenery,
the brain cuing up a sudden reel of beach, blue sky,
some nonsequitur of gentle wave upon wave
to coax the heart down from the height of its pounding.
That familiar way of seducing the dreamer:
this is the life, and it only gets better. Don't jump
back into the waking world just yet.

When people actually die in their sleep, it's nothing
they ever imagined happening to them. Not even remotely,
in their wildest dreams. They're out there on the edge
of the deepest breath of their lives,
in sleep so profound there's no analysis, no chance
of understanding later. And that has to hurt,
no matter what hope they stacked against hope,

as much as dying at high noon, fresh out of dreams
where against all odds of recurring circumstance
they go on living with a light on the nightstand,
a cool drink of water and someone at whatever door
delivering the promise we believed when we were small:
it's only a dream. How happy we used to be
to hear that, and in no time we'd feel ridiculously brave,
would be dead to the world all over again.

Those were the days we were going to live forever
and sometimes it still feels miraculously possible. Tonight
I might go over Niagara Falls in a barrel
snuggled up to the most beautiful woman in the world.
And chances are, if the wisdom holds, we'll make it,
we'll both live another day to tell anything we recall.
On mornings with the sun too fat and sassy in the window
it's no small wonder we're waking up at all,
coming even halfway back to our senses.
It's another day, the monster at the foot of the bed
that seems so real, so murderous,
so hungry it could eat every one of our dreams for breakfast.
And we open our eyes, remembering from last time how
we'll have to give it everything we've got.

Do Not Disturb

I guess someone finally thought that the words spoke for themselves.

—nightclerk explaining why so many hotel "do not disturb" signs have dropped the classic drawing of the Happy Sleeper

for the vanishing hero: R.I.P.

When it's been too many days in a row
of waking up for no good reason, too many times
of eyes wide open in a night that's got
a lot more dark to go, I think about that man
on those flimsy hotel room signs: DO NOT DISTURB.
He makes it look so easy.
Whenever you see him, he's in a nightshirt, buried
under covers, his thin smile barely visible.
His life is a tiny masterpiece of sleep.
He's dreaming another day's fresh towel on his face,
a new cake of soap full of lathery promise, one more
clean glass for whatever he's pouring. His whole world
can be made up in one unconscious blink, sanitized
for his protection. He's worked out this written deal
with the maid, his patron saint and silent partner.

But something in that fragile smile says it wasn't
always this way. There must be something
he's not telling, those first disquieting nights on the job
when a few ice cubes spit back into a glass or
a television stuttering its snowy goodnight
was enough to wake him out of one more dreamed-up life
where people meant it when they said DO NOT DISTURB
and into the noise of how little they really
had to be left alone to do.

I bet in his time he's heard it all
or heard enough: at least a hundred ways
the same dull ache revs up again in the heart,
tears backwards through the nerves
and shakes the brain out of its dozing.
And maybe he tried a few encouraging words
for the person inside, lost sleep of his own
when he realized he might as well be talking to
himself. I'd like to ask him how he finally did it,
how he learned to pull the shades and cut
the lights behind his eyes. Learned to sleep
right through his heart's white noise.
But there's no talking to him. For years
he's been sending a slender thread of Z's
into the air, his message that he's come to the end
of anything he could possibly have to say.

It's never the same at home without him
where the ashtray's always spilling over grey,
where I pick up the phone and no one gets on
to promise me the first line out. Some nights here
my life comes too easily undone alone in bed.
It might be days where nothing changes
and every night I climb back into
seems a little worse for sleeping than I left it.
That's when I fall back on the only faith around,
thin Gideons I've turned to so many times
I can quote chapter and verse without blinking:
the sullen fellowship of the bathroom mirror,
another finger of a drink I can still choke down,
the lucky shirt I'm saving for tomorrow.

Whatever it takes. Just ask the man next door.
For years he's been throwing open his attic window

and screaming at the Venusians to leave him alone.
I don't think he means a word he says.
Once he told me he can hear their voices
in the wind and don't get him wrong, he thinks
it's some kind of honor, but he's got better things
to do. Whenever I see him he's in his rocker,
looking for the slightest twitch of leaves.
With his fingertip wet in the air, he's almost
scientific. He carries on
the only way he knows without a prayer.

And now we'll have to do without the genuine DO NOT
DISTURB, without the ancient cartoon grace of that man
on the other side of the door, covering for us
in his insistent sleep, making us better
than we are. We'd be grateful for his help:
one whimsical promise. Some friendly osmosis.
It's clear my neighbor could use a sign. Sooner
or later we're all that anxious for the chance
to say *not now*, no matter how half-hearted,
no matter who it is we're only kidding.
These days I'd settle for the maid at any hour,
her cart bristling with ammonia and mops. Midnight,
noon, or 7 AM. I'd be a perfect gentleman
for as long as it took her to straighten out
my life, to do it up right for me again.
She wouldn't even know I was here. And for a minute
she might think I could finally be trusted
with one of those roomkeys people keep for souvenirs
until the day they forget why, until they remember
they can mail them back weeks, months, or years later,
for nothing, from anywhere else in the world.

Holding On

On any ring of keys we've ever carried,
no matter the size, there's always one that means
absolutely nothing. In all these years accumulating
like loose change that never adds up, of keeping things
private in so many different places, it's no wonder
we've drawn another sentimental blank: is this one
still useful? Or obsolete, a fossil? And we keep it
hanging around in some dark pocket of our lives
as if we'll wake up one morning suddenly wiser,
remembering foot lockers, strongboxes, diaries,
a warehouse on the outskirts, one night
locked in an embrace that went wrong in a hotel room,
a post office box, a top bureau drawer, a piece
of intricate machinery we operated once.

And sometimes, when just walking down the street
through one more day seems more than we can bear,
it might occur to us, that odd key out, its vestigial teeth
biting into the hip, rattling the purse,
chattering to its dimwitted cousins in the language
of keys. Whispering of a whole lost race,
a diaspora of keys, it breeds an unhealthy dissension.
Sooner or later they'll make their break, they'll be gone
for hours, days, weeks, a desperate chaingang of keys,
until they're found in the last place anyone would look
without a trace of remorse. And we'll know the ringleader:
a key among keys, but not *of* them.
Sometimes we get this easily carried away.

And maybe now we're on a street we've never seen,
as if it's leading us somewhere, daring us to keep pace,
like a key that's been around, that's seen its share
of keyhole. Like something that really knows a place
it could slip quietly into and turn for the better
with us right behind, holding on. Until we're in a room where
someone's getting ready for bed and asks what took us
so far out of our way to begin with, what kept us going
through those thin years since. A room that's been made up
almost to perfection, with only one thing
missing. And at last that's where we come in.
Maybe above this storefront. Or in that apartment house
next door. Or where the freight elevator heaves and rises,
humming our name all the way to the top.

This key must have been important. An honor
and a privilege. Even now it vaguely reminds us of a time
we could be trusted that much. That far. With something.
We keep meaning to get rid of it, but it's hard
to throw away a key. It's the threat no one ever makes
good on: *I'm gonna lock the door and. . . .*We are given only
so many in a life. And despite the ways
they weigh us down or hold us up fumbling through them
in the dark, feeling for the lock, it's never enough.

So on a day like today we have to feel lucky
that we're short a vital padlock, a gate swinging open,
an honorary city. We may be worn out, may be rubbed smooth,
but we've still got the smallest of reserves jangling
in our imagination. We're waiting for just the right moment
and place, waiting to be let in on the secret
other side of the door where what we've been
carrying around so long finally fits and makes sense
and we didn't walk by our chance this time, never dreaming.

America's Bed-and-Breakfasts

for G. Barnes, who really did try to book me into something a little more my style

i.

Even though I'm only staying the night, I have a sinking feeling
there's going to be trouble. The real guests are talking it up in the living room
as if this is truly the life: what more could people want, this far from home,
than to have every bit of their weariness and hunger taken so personally? Why
would anyone settle for less? When they checked in and filled out the card
with way too much space for *Tell Us All About Yourself,* I bet they were more
than happy to oblige. I can hear them even now, while I'm writing down
the only thing I'm sure of, after my name and my actual address:
I can already tell there's no way I deserve this kind of attention.

I travel for the thrill of asserting what I can't be expected to know.
Because I enjoy the molecular rearrangement that being a stranger occasions,
I don't necessarily want to feel as if I'm somehow fitting into
the familiar chambers of my life one more time. It's as if my Aunt Ida suddenly
was named the nation's hotelier, and from now on there'll be no such thing as
too much potpourri, too many of those giant ceramic pitchers on hallway tables,
dried flowers sprouting from the mouths of all the usual antiques in the land.
Aunt Ida in St. Louis, Salt Lake City, Sausalito, New Orleans. Aunt Ida
beckoning from every porch swing throughout charm-smitten New England.

ii.

It's not enough that this place has taken its name from some official roster
of the Atmospherically Correct. Each room has its own ambiance spelled out:
The Salt Air. The Espresso. The Battle-of-Gettysburg Room. And there's no
Major Hoople from my Sunday funnies childhood showing me the way, guiding star

of *Our Boarding House* in his resplendent fez, kaff-kaffing through adventure
after unlikely adventure. No. My hosts are gentle Dick and Jane, grown serious
and pale after too many years of rehabbing their straight-and-narrow world.

Ten minutes of this and my own color's fading. I'm already losing sleep
I haven't even thought of yet. I'm actually on my knees, despairing in front of
the shelf or two of books they insist on calling The Library: soil conservation,
too-local histories, the requisite wisdom of Edgar Guest. I grab the Boy Scouts
Survival Handbook because now the other guests are chummied up around the piano,
lost in a spirited medley of show tunes, and I'm afraid it can only get worse:
some trigger-happy soul's bound to pull out a guitar, squeeze off a few rounds
of *Michael, Row the Boat Ashore*. And then it's *Kumbaya* before you know it.

iii.

Now I'm turning my polite version of a pillow over and over, looking for
the cool side. I'm really expected to sleep through this night, to wake up
for breakfast: fresh-squeezed juice and something like scones, a china cup
of exotic decaffeinated coffee while all these slap-happy pilgrims talk about
what's next. The Eichorns will be, as always, irrepressible. They're excited
about meandering through another Farmers' Market. Nancy and Donna can't wait
to be in a boat on the lake. And Dick and Jane might smile and wonder out loud
what could possibly be in store for Mr. Misanthrope. As if I didn't have
enough to answer for already.

                    I can dream, can't I? There's a sleepy
1950s aqua-trimmed motel, its VACANCY still radiant in neon.
The guy at the night desk doesn't want to talk about politics or love, much less
about his hula girl tattoo. He doesn't give a damn if I'm in town
on legitimate business, on the lam, on account of any sunburned Donna.
And the unassuming key he hands over lets me into The Cradle-of-Civilization-
As-I've-Come-to-Know-It Room, where I kick off my shoes with impunity
and warm up the TV, caressing its lovely rabbit ears. It's my kind of night

already. Later I'm walking the grounds with that plastic bucket in my hands,
drawn to the all-night humming of the ice machine, its cold beauty
the surest sustenance around. In moments I'll have something to carry with me
for as long as it lasts. Something finally to give away when people come asking.
And I can get more if I have to. I can give them all they want.

iv.

Because sometimes it's hard to remember exactly
who you are, what you're doing anywhere. That's when I least believe in
talking it out or sleeping it off or passing it around a table like bread again
until everyone's had his fill. And even if we're supposed to feel like part of
the same ridiculous family, no matter how big, how impossibly happy, I can't imagine
for the life of me why people would choose to make themselves so much at home
that they're perfectly willing to sing along through endless verses full of
those same monotonous assurances: that no one's a stranger
to suffering, but neither will we be strangers forever to the blessings
that seem a little far away right now. OK, so maybe
just one more time: *River Jordan is chilly and wide. . . .*

Bed-and-Breakfast on the other side.

From the Other Side, Houdini Tries to Come Through for Bess

I wish I could make a promise so cocky
there'd be no doubt: you'd know that act anywhere.
I'd like to give you an answer we both could live with
forever, but if you want to know the truth,
I'm still not sure. I guess that sounds like me
all over again, those early days you suggested marriage.
I finally came around. And now this tricky question
of an Afterlife. I need more time to get it right.
Nights on end you're probably awake, waiting for me
to make up my mind once more. I don't want you to hear
the news, either way, from anyone else. So don't listen
to any two-bit medium who swears he's the one
who's broken through, received the promised message
from your husband. No more scams in ectoplasm.
No more candles in the breezeway. And please, no more
table knocking so heavy-handed that the Fox sisters,
wherever they are, must be unbelievably sorry
they ever left the business. These psychics see a future
where it's easy dollars in their pockets and hundreds
of new miles on tour if you give them even an inch of
it could *be Harry*. It won't ever be me
mumbling through those pawnshop trumpets, announcing
myself with those timid little bells. I've got
a reputation I wear like a jacket I actually swim in:
always larger than life.

Remember when we lay together in our double-jointed love,
the adrenaline of the Hippodrome, that closing night finale
still pumping through us, the bed levitating

just to keep up with our new heights of dexterity?
We brought out the best we had, bright-colored scarves
of caring without end, from deep within each other.
And drifting back down into the mortal world again,
the unembellished Bess and Harry, we struck that crazy deal
we laughed about less as we watched each other
growing slowly older: whoever passed over first would try
to get a message back to the other. Because we wanted it
to go on forever, even though we never saw a shred
of living proof. Well, there's no escaping the obvious:
I'm first, and I never felt this completely lost before
in my life. I don't know where or what in the world.
When I close my eyes, things seem a little too familiar:
the dark must of another crate they'd like to see me
never leave, one more tight spot someone's devised
with an eye toward tomorrow's early edition. It's the same
black swaddling I was born to greatness in, and I'm here

to say I need your veteran patter, your unerring sense
of misdirection before I can make good again. So good
whole continents know my name. Remember the Milk Can?
The chained trunk in the East River? The German jails
where I sat naked, straitjacketed and cuffed, behind
a makeshift veil of curtains? Just as the proper pall
fell over the audience, I made sure to get out alive.
Even when I read your mind, caught you thinking maybe
it won't work, not this time, you still managed your best
assistant's smile. The smile of the long-married-
to-disaster-waiting-to-happen, smile that floats to the top
of another sinking feeling. I kept meaning to tell you
how easy it was, knowing you were waiting there
on the other side of whatever dark. It was your name, too,
on the line every time: Houdini. When you held your breath
for us both, it was your sympathetic death-defying
magic that never failed to bring me back.

Hard to top an act of love like that. And what's worse,
I've got a gut feeling this is different from vanishing
an elephant on stage, from picking locks,
slipping manacles and chains. Or from nonchalantly
walking through a wall and reappearing on the other side
of the footlights. It's darker than it used to be
between us, Bess, and I don't think I can talk myself
out of here alone. I need another Houdini.
I'll be wearing that suit I wore to our wedding. It's still
a good fit, even after more than a thousand performances
of public husband, public wife. And I'll never forget
that kiss we closed every show with, the sure-fire
way it opened up like a trap-door just in time,
the bottom falling out of everything that seemed
so impossibly mystifying in the rest of my life.

If you're still holding out for something more substantial,
ask yourself who else could deliver the words we swore
we'd never have to use again, save for maybe
this one performance only. And who else could tell you
exactly where to find them: your anniversary strongbox,
underneath my mother's brooch, at the end of the letter
I mailed you from Paris and the last solo tour
I ever willingly took on: *the human heart's too tough
a room to work alone.* That has a Douglas Fairbanks ring
I couldn't muster for Hollywood love or money
in those motion pictures you tried to talk me out of.
I've always been better live, in person, thriving
on the audible disbelief of the crowd. Now I'm dreaming

of staging the comeback of a lifetime. With your assistance.
I'm dreaming you closer, working your way through
the sweetest letters of the alphabet: SRO.
Because we're still magic. Our act still packs them in.
When you knock on the lid to demonstrate once

and for all how sturdy, how uncompromising, it's a code:
how many more minutes or hours or years. The trick is
in letting the suspense build until it nearly kills them.
We called it Metamorphosis or Buried Alive, depending
on the finish we thought they'd least expect.

Those years of practice taught us nothing solid ever
really disappears. Sooner or later, though,
that's how it has to seem to everyone, no matter
how closely they're watching or what they honestly believe.
We were that good, Bess. Our whole life. We lived
for those nights when our love was the only show in town
and the people rose out of their seats to let us know
we'd done it again. And you knew more than they did.
You knew *how.* Now they see it,
now they don't. Because the hand is only quicker than
the untrained eye looking in every wrong direction.

You've got to keep tonight's implausible secret
where it's always been: just between you and me. Now
it's assurance, now it's tenuous wishing,
a thread stretched tight between paper cups when really
one of us should be sleeping, the other not making
a sound. And suddenly we're this young again, Houdini
calling Houdini with nothing but love on the line.
Believe me when I tell you if a candle flame flickers
by the side of your bed, a small eternity away
from the claptrap of the seance, the dimestore manifestations,
it's a kiss blown across the whole unlikely distance
that no one can say for sure actually appeared
or disappeared, like nothing else can, into thin air.

II. The Protocol of Desire

The kiss of death is currently prohibited by law. Look for it in later editions.

—Kenneth Koch, *The Art of Love*

The Anatomy of Wishful Thinking

i.

An instinct coded generations deep in the genes
says this makes wishing better, makes it work more
surely. We get the message early on, how we're only
human. And so we close our eyes.
We believe in the eyelid's genuflection
there's something that cinches the deal we make with whatever fate
blows our way. Blow out the candles and we open our eyes
to a few puffs of smoke and some cheap applause. It's easy
magic. An honest piece of cake.

Real prayer takes growing into. Those eventual days
when the world wells up or funnels down to precious
little, we light candles in rooms too small to live in.
We fold our hands until the knuckles go white
with concentration, close our eyes and imagine everything
we'd say out loud if anyone were there to hear us.
We're asking for the moon again, but we'd settle for
the tiniest sliver of light we could point to
in a picture of days on the horizon, better than what's really
hanging cockeyed on the walls we've been meaning to paint over.

Or say for once when we open our eyes there's someone else
sitting with us on the edge of the bed, here to see us through
a night too dark for prayer, and now's our chance
to get reacquainted with the protocol of desire, how the eyes
close again over a kiss, over love even deeper,
lower down than that. And so we take the headlong plunge,
the blind faith of the desperate believer. But we can always feel it

slipping away, clearing its throat, stealing into the hall
where it keeps on going. And we just can't bring ourselves
to open our eyes. It's nothing we haven't seen before.

Taken to extreme, it's sleep. Unconscious wishing hours on end.
Conceding another day's played out and what's needed, really
needed, is the strength to summon one more starting over.
We can believe in tomorrow. We want it in the worst way,
the sun staring in through the window until we wake up, eyes
stinging, trying to rub out whatever dream's
burned itself into the retina this time. Trying to bring
the sharp edges of the world into focus again. Or else
we're thinking how it could be even worse, and so we close our eyes:
just a few more minutes. A way of saying *not yet*
or *we couldn't be more ready.*

And to its logical conclusion: dying. Then it's Close the Eyes
and Pull the Sheet Up Over the Head. That's the way
we used to sleep, more often than not, but surely
this is more. It's Lay On the Coins. It's Over the River.
It's We'll Never Get Out of These Woods.

ii.

When a small child closes his eyes, he's going
on sheer reflexive nerve. He thinks suddenly
he's invisible there on the floor, pale
peek-a-boo moon barely breathing,
learning the darker side of his *pretty please* devotions:
please don't. Not now. Not me. Ask him and he'd say
he's just playing. But he really believes
that because he can't see, no one and nothing can find him either.
He's going through that phase where there's no distinction yet

between himself and the rest of the charted world, he feels that much
a part of things for now.

That's a ticklish give-and-take we'd like
never to let go of. But it's wishful thinking that asks more
and more for some kind of giving up: pennies in the fountain,
fireflies hurled back into the night. It's milkweed or feathers
or this year's fairy dust, the fragile wisps of things.
It's a falling star trailing its tiny thread of light
and one more day on the planet unravels in a single blink.
It's the bone snapped in two when the wishing's over
and we open our eyes to see how it's come apart this time
in our hands. Even then it's hard to remember: is it big
or little has its way? With us it's never easy, always somewhere
between the rock and Hell. The hard place. The high water.
And the cardinal rule of wishing: you can never tell.

These last few minutes this poem's all you've had,
and maybe you've been waiting for a bit more reassurance. Now
you understand: that's wishful thinking, the hum
these words have been riding on. OK.
Let's turn up that music. Imagine a sympathetic jazzman
blowing so low, so sure between these lines
that you know without looking his eyes are closed
and where he's coaxing that music from is beyond you.
He'll carry on until he runs out of breath
and has to come up again into the floodlight of the world for air.
Then comes that dream we've all had versions of
too many times. In this one he's calling you
up to the stand. You're holding a horn brighter than anything
you've ever seen, and there's no time to tell anyone
you don't play. Or at least not since you were a kid.
So close your eyes. You can never tell. Somewhere
there's got to be music. Let's see what you can do.

What Some People Won't Do

If I'm supposed to be doing the laundry
and you're supposed to be doing the cooking, then what
are we doing here in the bedroom at 4 in the afternoon?
So much to be done, and we're getting it exactly
backwards: I'm undoing your blouse. You're undoing my serious buckle.
You'd think we'd grow up for once in our lives
the way so many others seem to do—people who don't even
for a minute think of jumping into those neat piles of leaves
they've spent the whole day raking.

Days like this we're doing the best we can. Sooner or later
we reach that point where there's nothing left to do
or undo. We come smack up against the inviolable
laws of physics, or else we're simply that exhausted, done in
first by the weightlessness, then the unexpected gravity of love.

Part of me wants to say as usual this is all
your doing, but I don't: Monk's *I Mean You* on the stereo
was my idea this time. I know what that tune does to you.
I'm adding to a list of things that won't get done, and you
are nowhere on it. Believe me, there are moments when I realize
precisely what I'm doing.
                                   And whenever I imagine my life
without you in it, doing the difficult work of love you do so well—
the grace without end, the heavy lifting of forgiveness,
the most demanding of the 101 positions—I come unabashedly
undone. Sometimes I get so unreasonably happy
I don't know what else to do. That's when I need you
doing the sweet-talking for us both. Until part of me's whispering again

to that part of you that won't be outdone, and suddenly we're taking it
once more from the top, Thelonious doing his *Straight, No Chaser* now.

Our much-too-responsible neighbor who hates the music we play
will stop his own backbreaking work in the yard just long enough
to shake his head, certain that somehow we've done him wrong,
that he's discovered a fly in the soup the world's dished out
for him today: what's the meaning of this, exactly what do we think
we're doing, unasked for this afternoon in his made-to-order life?
Without missing a beat, we'd like to say *the backstroke,*
but we've got to stop falling back on vaudeville, especially
if we ever hope to be as good as the next guy at yardwork
or plumbing or walking the dog—whatever needs serious doing.

As far as love's concerned, we're industrious to a fault:
we have absolutely nothing to wear, no supper to sit down to.
But we're so good at making do, we have to laugh:
another day it's impossible to feel the least bit sorry
for everything we've gone and done again.

But Seriously

99.2% of Americans claim they can't tell a joke to save their lives.

 —Harper's Index

i. *Don't Rush Me:*

A woman goes to the doctor. No,
wait. She calls the doctor instead. She doesn't go.
She's not the one who's sick. It's her husband. That's what
she tells the doctor. Sort of: *he thinks he's a*
refrigerator. See, she can't help thinking about what
he's thinking. But it's not the same. Wait. Not *a refrigerator;*
a chicken. The doctor asks if that's a real problem.
Not that it isn't *real*, really, but is it a *problem?*
For either of them, he's thinking. It may not be the same.
Well, he snores when he sleeps, and that little light
keeps me awake all night. No, wait. I mean the doctor
hears *a chicken,* says it's no big deal, he's heard worse
and promises to have her husband back to himself
in no time. And the woman says *could you take a little longer?*
I don't want the milk to go bad. No. I mean
chicken. She says *chicken* to the doctor back there
near the beginning, about what her husband thinks.
Forget the snoring. Mostly she sleeps fine. And trust me,
no one in this story's about to cry over spoiled milk.
I don't even know where that *refrigerator* came from.
The exasperated doctor takes no joy in shouting *Sears.*
It's funny: the woman who started this seems worried
more than ever, and suddenly I guess it's all of us
who really need the eggs about now.

ii. *I'll End Up Getting This* . . .

A kangaroo walks into a bar in Chicago
and orders a Harvey Wallbanger. The bartender acts astonished,
as if he's never heard of a kangaroo in a bar before.
The kangaroo smiles, knocks it back, asks how much she owes.
The bartender's sure this must be some kind of joke:
25 dollars should do it. As the kangaroo reaches into her pouch,
the bartender, a creature of habit himself, can't resist: *you know,*
we don't get many kangaroos in here. But the kangaroo's
not as dumb as she looks. She's heard this one before, heard it
all her drinking life. She pulls out a sawed-off .22
and shoots the bartender dead. *It's a changing eco-system,*
it's airline deregulation, and she lets herself out, laughing.
Even the drunk at the end of the bar knows
this isn't how it's supposed to go, but still, he's not
all that surprised: *it's no wonder, at these prices.*

A kangaroo walks into a bar in St. Louis.

iii. . . . *Completely Backwards*

It's almost enough to make him laugh.
Now his only problem is he's fifty miles from home.
It worked like a dream: he feels like almost
another man completely. Ten days later he calls the doctor,
who asks if there's been any dramatic improvement.
The doctor can assure him five miles a day
might change everything. He really should consider running.
The doctor can't find any organic explanation.
The man doesn't believe in doctors, but maybe just this once.
He's worried. It's something to do with his heart.
His best dreams have lost their color, and even his own face
today is nearly disappearing in the mirror.
He has to do something. He aches for no good reason.
Like milk in a refrigerator. A man wakes up one morning someplace
he's never been in his life before, and it comes to him
out of nowhere: how far things can go bad, how quietly
and for how long. It goes like this. I might not get it exactly
right, but have you heard the one about the man who hopes
someone lets him in on the joke before it's over?

The Final Meeting of the Pessimists Club

I can promise you this much:
it will be that philosophic glass-of-water question
does them in, whenever. The full-blooded optimist in me
says it could happen tonight. We'll have to see

how it goes for the lovers halfway across town,
pressing their lips together so completely, for a moment
there's only one luxurious mouth where it's safe to say
they can speak their hearts. When they come apart to catch a breath:

the sound of a cork popping loose from a bottle,
and the moon begins its slow rising before their eyes, a bubble
that will take the better part of this night at least
to get where it's going. Their love's that deep, and sometimes

they feel the pressure. I promise: they're in that far
over their heads again. And wobbly with celebration.
Say they knew what was coming, but didn't think
it would be nearly this quick in getting here.

Measured against the reckless speed of light, love takes
its own sweet time. They were used to the slow days, clothes
coming off button by reliable button.
Tonight she's in a dress so red it seems unlikely

she'll be talked out of it, but you never know. Just now
she might have found it in herself to be this brave,
to keep it on a little longer. After all, he gets to wear
that audacious hat he'd never own up to in broad daylight.

And if you're waiting, impatient, if you were just wondering,
we can go back across town to the banquet hall
where the members of the Pessimists Club are equally restless:
the keynote speaker from Dubuque's a good hour overdue

and the idiotic busboy's actually whistling
on his brisk walk back into the miseries of the kitchen.
He's carrying what's left of a hundred chicken dinners
and seems so unnaturally happy whenever someone stops him

and asks would it be possible to get some more water?
OK. Who's he to say no? He'll be right back.
Because by now surely the lovers are singing softly to each other,
skin to skin, fragile instruments of each other's desire

and all the delicate fingerings. If the music they're making
between them like sudden virtuosos in the grass
sounds too good to be true, I'm here to tell you it isn't.
Too good to be true, I mean. There's no denying: desire's made up

of yes and no, depending. But mostly, I'd say yes.
Yes, here comes the busboy with the water. Here come the lovers
pouring sweat. Everyone's timing is impeccable for once.
The busboy's racing from table to table, tipping that pitcher

for all he's worth. And he's as out of breath as the lovers.
A night of breathing in the extreme, and everyone looks up: the moon's
half-full. Tonight, like it or not, that's how they see it.
Half-a-slipper's worth of pale champagne.

A couple of them will be out there tomorrow night too, their love
grown one day fatter on its axis. Were he a writer, or she,
I'd say there'd be some eloquent waxing in the air.
And each would know exactly what the other was about

to say: it's no wonder you can't have it all
in a single instant. Every night there's a little more, and more
to look forward to. It's crazy that it works that way,
that no one knows any more about it than The Man

in the Moon. In a few nights he's bound to be there indisputably
for you. Positively luminous, shining and finally whole,
his life no longer a dull coin turned over and over
in a dark pocket, vaguely wished on, rubbed for some nebulous luck.

It's just the configuration of the lunar peaks and valleys
makes him look that certain way, where things have hit and finally
sunk in far enough to make a lasting impression, and still
he'll be glowing when you meet him face to face.

And the busboy too, and those he's been serving so wisely.
Now in the hall the crowd's rising as one, this fraternity of worry
no more, leaving behind a hundred glasses of water
decidedly, startlingly fuller than empty, wondering

what's the worst that could happen when they feel this good,
half-satisfied, half-looking forward? The busboy, the ex-
pessimists minus their gloomy fezzes, and the lovers
imagining the full moon ahead. Maybe especially the lovers:

they can see it right now. They find hard to believe
any kind of life on the dark side, where even as I speak
the lost bus from Dubuque's pulling in without a single passenger.
We've all waited long enough: for tonight, not a nay-sayer anywhere.

She Dreamed She Was Writing a Love Poem

There's a word for that last impulsive quiver in the leg,
those few cells still cruising the night on sheer nerve.
A word for the tongue's unconscious flutter between her lips,
for the delicate envelope of sleep she's folding herself into
to be opened slowly, handled with care tomorrow, with any luck
one more love letter on the loose in a blushing world.
But exactly where she's headed tonight no one but she can say.

If a few of her own words slip out along the way,
she'll never know what she's missing. She can't hear them
above the hum of the fan, can't see them rising in balloons
over the improbable heroine's head in living Sunday color.

There's so much she has to say, it's not funny.
It's exhausting, this breaking down even a single day
into its tiny constituent bits, charged particles
of the unexpected or the familiar or worse in a field
no bigger than a moment. And in the crucial act of naming them,
getting them right out loud, she's distributing the undeniable
facts of another day's atomic weight, making it somehow
bearable and real. She can't wait to get started
living by words again. It's always a precarious sunrise
she's talking herself into. And she's getting good,
even if she does have to say so, dreamily, herself:

it's Junior High shop class, sawdust and goggles,
Mr. Kunkel in his grey industrial apron, and she's finished
the requisite spice rack, the flimsy picture frame.
She's killing time in her notebook, casually raising a Taj Mahal
out of language: words, sturdy and reliable enough

to put the rest of that day into. She'd carry it unassumingly
in syllables of heartbeat, in the elemental grammar of breathing.
Her classmates, their mouths full of actual nails, are applauding
and Mr. Kunkel's losing control. He needs a smoke about now.

And in the morning it might dawn on her all at once: breeze
through the kitchen window, toast rising golden,
that first drop of sweet cream getting lost in her coffee:
this life like a plum bursting cool in her mouth,
a pleasure so palpable it's all over her face.
She'll wonder if there's a single word for that.

She's laughing now, finally, in her fragile sleep:
here she is again, examining atom by preposterous atom
what's happened and what hasn't yet, polar opposites
lying down together in the same improbable bed
while they whisper their more scientific names
in her discerning ear.
                         She's beside herself with wonder,
and that makes everything twice as exciting, twice
as disturbing for the man who's been mere inches from her, awake
this whole while, listening hard the way anxious people will
through radio static. Those people on the verge of
discovering something big if only the signal holds long enough:
where the fire was, when the bad weather's coming, why the woman
on the phone-in sounds so worried, how many lives
already are feared lost. And if there's any music, maybe
they'll find out who in her right mind would be singing
at a time like this. And the one good reason she could have:
whatever in the world for.

She's putting her fingers to his lips now, as if
he's been the one doing the talking. There has to be a word
for that kind of telepathic power. There's a lot to be said

for his sudden smile, his furious scribbling in the dark,
how he'll never sleep until he hears the promise and
gets it in writing: just one more of those ridiculous names
his love insists on going by this time.

Lessons in Another Language

i.

The first lesson in any language makes it seem really
possible. After just a few minutes we felt almost at home
in the extremes of *hello* and *goodbye*. We repeated them
back to back, the natural order of things abridged, as if to say
yes, we know exactly what we're in for. It was too early to tell
about anything we should be doing in-between, how much and how
much harder that could possibly be. When we gave up
our good names for the new ones ringing strangely
in our parochial ears, we were just beginning to understand
how long it might take to learn our fluent way around.

We still relied on gestures, quick pictures in the thin air
of everything we wanted to say. We could have used some encouraging
words, but they didn't occur to us that soon. So it was *hello*
to the hair, *hello* to the cheek, *hello* until the neurons whispered
their own rendition: a gentle rippling down the spine.
And we were nervous in spite of the swagger in the hands
their first time out on those international waters.

Something told us we'd catch on: we'd do it in the dark,
do it with our hands tied behind our backs, dressed in only
our sophisticated voices, every superfluous article dropping away
until we were face to face with undreamed-of nouns
and all the untranslatable, luxuriant verbs they lead to.
We'd listen to the nuance of skin on skin, every ruddy inflection,
the unflinching accent mark the tongue lays down in salt.

And repeat: lip and tongue and tooth positioned this way
and that. Holding our breath until we were sure we could make it
look easy, an absolute breeze: every intimate plosive
set to go off in the mouth of this new language.

ii.

No matter how many years of conscientious study, thousands
of new words later, there are going to be some embarrassing moments,
even a few notorious mistakes like those kind in restaurants
where what's already steaming and headed our way looks like
trouble we would swear we didn't ask for.

And try as we may to be urbane, taking our polite turns
doing the talking, trying to undo what came out inexplicably wrong
by sending it back immediately into the heat of some far-flung kitchen,
what comes out now are all those idiotic phrasebook questions,
standard issue for the cartoon tourist much too far from home:
When is the next train out of town? Could you please pass
the time? Does love last longer as an abstract noun
or transitive verb? And isn't the weather as good as we could hope for?

Whenever we get that flustered in each other's company,
we'd like to point to anyone in the middle of a romantic dinner—
candles, chablis, crepes folded just so—and say
we'd like exactly what they're having over there. Figuratively
speaking, of course. There's no one else in the room.
Even the imperious waiter shaking his head and sighing is only
wishful thinking, an idea someone's trying to portion out in words
to keep from going completely to pieces. A last split-second effort
to grab the wine glass on its tense, irretrievable way to the floor.

It seems there are days we've forgotten everything we learned.
That's when we fall back on native intelligence: a kiss
in the rain or a fire in the fireplace of our rented bungalow until
most of it comes back to us: the idioms rekindled,
the local customs of our eccentric province honored again
in the common tongue, and *hello,* we're sweet-talking
one more private lesson there will be no paying for
ever, no matter how bright the coin, how generous
and how suddenly enormous the realm.

Vegetarian Physics

The tofu that's shown up overnight in this house is frightening
proof of the Law of Conservation: matter that simply cannot be
created or destroyed. Matter older than Newton,
who knew better than to taste it. Older than Lao-tzu,
who thought about it but finally chose harmonious non-interference.
I'd like to be philosophical too, see it as some kind of pale
inscrutable wisdom among the hot dogs, the cold chicken,
the leftover deviled eggs, but I'm talking curdled
soybean milk. And I don't have that kind of energy.

I'd rather not be part of the precariously metaphorical
wedding of modern physics and the ancient Eastern mysteries.
But still: whoever stashed the tofu in my Frigidaire
had better come back for it soon. I'm not Einstein
but I'm smart enough to know a bad idea when I see it
taking up space, biding its time.
Like so much that demands our imperfect attention
amid the particle roar of the world: going nowhere, fast.

I Can't Believe the Face on Mars

for Patricia

Some guy's bought half an hour of TV time to talk about a photo
beamed back by the Viking probe over the red plains of Cydonia where,
to hear him tell it, an ancient Martian race has painstakingly fashioned
a monumental human face. It's 2 AM and he isn't saying why,
but he's hawking his homemade book about what has to be, he insists, *the most*
amazing find of the millennium. And because I can't believe the face on Mars
is anything more than a freakish accident of light and shadow, I guess
I'm getting hopelessly old.
                              As a kid I took it all as gospel: UFOs, Abominable
Snowmen, Atlantis, ESP, ghosts. But especially UFOs—I wanted to imagine
some other life possible worlds away from this one. I needed something
flying in the face of the Ordinary, so I believed at once in everything
inexplicable and in nothing I might actually have to get used to:
arithmetic, piano lessons, religion. Undeniable love.

These days we're mostly so sophisticated it's frightening.
We've got acres of the latest radio telescopes scanning the heavens
for the same old miraculous sign, pitch-perfect computerized signals
going out by the thousands, wave after differentiated wave, into the vast
desolation of space, just on the off chance of discovering that finally
we are not alone. All that, and my Martian scholar friend can't see me
making my own faces, can't hear me sighing out loud in my living room.
It's unmistakable, the desperation in his face that says we spend our lives
looking for clues that might give us enough to go on. But we always see more
or less than what we want to: in the extravagant night sky,
in photos from millions of miles away, in the smoky haze
of whatever rooms we're up too late in again. It might as well be
my father's face, all business, the telltale serious crease in the brow.

In the few grainy photos I have of him, he's somewhere in the grey hills
of Pennsylvania stiffly posing, off by himself, looking as if
he'd rather be anywhere else right now, forever.

The off-camera voice assures me: the face I should be seeing close up now
stretches over a mile of rugged terrain, clearly a sign of constructive,
intelligent life: a fierce, enigmatic labor of love. It's obvious this face
has become his whole life. No wonder it seems so long. No wonder
I can barely make out anything at all.
                                        It pales next to the exuberant faces
of those flying saucer zealots in the Fifties: George Adamski, Van Tassel,
Orfeo Angelucci, Howard Menger. I couldn't get enough of their colorful
antic tales of contact with actual flying saucer pilots who'd travelled from
unbelievable places just to deliver some cornball message to all humanity
through these even-more-unlikely, accidental Earthling go-betweens. It happened
almost always telepathically. Whether landing in Newark or the middle-of-
nowhere California desert, they didn't have to say a word.

But their fledgling emissaries had to, in treatise
after crackpot treatise: how they never saw it coming, they never
asked for it: the improbable physics, the mysterious gestures,
the hyperbolic beauty of the female crew that always somehow managed to figure
in their breathless recountings. And although invariably they were left
to take the long walk back to their roominghouses,
to their penny-ante labors, they honestly seemed to believe themselves
less alone. And being only human, they had to talk about it, in *Secret
of the Saucers* and *Inside the Space Ships. From Outer Space to You.*
In wild-eyed books with their own amazing faces staring out from the covers.

With time running out, the guy trying to sell me the Martian face
turns into every salesman in the world who senses the door slamming shut.
He resorts to the quick pitch: *seeing is believing.* But I bet he understands
it usually works, the other way around, like this: probably I'm seeing things
I've gone too long without. And because I believe they're finally possible again,

they are undeniably here. No spectral head of Elvis. No Scottish lake monsters
or out-of-focus Bigfoot. At the moment I can't even summon up the face
of a single waitress who ever said she'd be right back with more coffee
in my lifetime. But I have been seeing more of those flashing lights,
those odd shapes moving at impossible speeds, the unidentified flying objects
of love coming in quietly for a landing through the dark my life's been lately.
And now it's the fabled beam of light from the vicinity of the bedroom
and you, stepping suddenly out of it, radiant in your skin.

Even if it's true they never saw it coming, I think Adamski and the rest
had to be asking for *something*, secretly at least, at night
with no one else around—surely no less a version of prayer than any other.
In the desert, in the woods, in a deserted New Jersey industrial park
they offered it up in the general direction of heaven
and they couldn't wait for some kind of answer in the thick of their lives.
Let's face it: when the answer came to them, no matter how far-fetched,
yes, they were surprised. But not completely.
                                        And if those saucer disciples
were right about the telepathic powers, then you're sure to be thinking
what I'm thinking: where you've come from is less important by far
than what we're climbing into, headed wherever now. I'm on board
for the long haul. The giddy light-years. No matter the unlikely physics.
No matter the complex machinery, the inexplicable engines of the heart.

Finally I'm getting the benevolent message directly: sometimes
we are not alone. It almost got lost in those saucer books amid the vagaries
of love and Universal Understanding, the convoluted discussions of how
we might yet be saved, and just in time, from some worst part of ourselves.
No beings ever could have travelled all that way thinking any of this
would be easy. They must have hoped against hope they'd be lucky enough
to find the one person in the world this time who, believe it
or not, would believe it when he met them face to face.

Maybe that's all the guy on TV's wanted. He's just gone off the air
but a toll-free number keeps flashing, as if he'll be up all night knowing
what he knows, and how can anyone else sleep either?
Last night I watched you sleeping, illumined in the streetlight
through the bedroom window, our reliable neighborhood moon. And for a minute
I couldn't believe the grace in your cheekbones, your flickering eyes,
the gentle slope of your chin right under that otherworldly smile.
I couldn't believe my own eyes. I had to touch you to make sure
you simply *were,* that it wasn't just me in the leftover light
from stars no longer actually themselves in the sky.
And it wasn't just me: the entire universe took a deep breath,
let it slowly out again. An astronomical sigh of relief.

What could it hurt to call and tell him yes, if it means
so much to him, he's right, there is a face on Mars beyond the shadow
of a doubt. I never really meant to believe otherwise. At least
I can see that much now.

III. Lost in the Fire

Lost in the Fire

This localization of terrific heat in a body, yet not extending to flammable objects nearby, is the great mystery of SHC—Spontaneous Human Combustion.

—Vincent Gaddis, *Mysterious Fires and Lights*

i. A Starter Kit

When it's a storage shed, garage, nightmare of an attic
or one more derelict warehouse lit up in the night
and authorities can't find any neighborhood kid
with his pocket full of matches and a bad idea,
we might have to settle for the textbook explanation:
rags and gasoline, the invariably poor ventilation, heat
gradually building to the delicate point of ignition and
suddenly it's a plausible last resort: spontaneous combustion.

The smallest leap of faith should tell us it can happen
this way too: people burn, it's humanly possible
and for no good reason experts can agree on, burn
in minutes from the inside out with something so hot
it takes people who burn for a living, professionals
at their incinerators, hours of patient stoking
to achieve that degree of obliteration.

If you're a physician in the 17th century you've decided
by now: *the long and immoderate use of Spiritous Liquors.*
Firewater and White Lightning. Smoking Skull
and Boilermaker. Small wonder, then, the number of folks
lit up all over the world.
The woman in the grocery line checks out the latest theory:
UFO aliens detonating their overgrown science homework

through a kind of remotely fiendish mind control.
In the coroner's office they've always been fond of *death
by misadventure,* hinting at some vague, misguided bravery.
In centuries of monasteries it's a matter of pious record
where, being eternal optimists, they called it The Fire
from Heaven. When it struck, it struck completely down.

Historically, incredibly and simply: people have burned.
And they will burn again. They'll flame and sear
until there's no more fire left in them, until it goes out
without touching another single thing in the cold-water flats
of their lives. Until what's left is essence, a scattering
of blackened DNA, a residue on the floorboards
while the curtains continue to blow. While their chairs
and the tables they set remain undaunted, anticipating
the arrival of some altogether splendid company.

Maybe it's the twisted inverse of the ballyhooed lightning
that charged the planet's primordial soup
and just the right amino acids twitched into recognizable life.
When however many eons later something crawled out of the water,
discovered fire on the beach and told stories around it all night,
convinced this was a step in the right direction:

ii. A Royal Fairy Tale

Once upon a time in 1836 in Cesena, Italy, the Countess Cornelia di Bandi spent three hours talking with her maid. As Countesses often do, she spoke only about herself: her accomplishments and her dreams. She dismissed the maid when it finally grew late enough to say her prayers—the prayers of everyone but small children at bedtime being mostly private matters. God only knows what she must have prayed for exactly, in a Countess's version of prayer. All we can say for sure: now she lay her down to sleep.

The next morning the maid became worried when she wasn't summoned at the usual hour. Eventually she mustered the courage to mount the stairs, all the while wondering what words she should use to wake her mistress. Her deliberation was cut short by the sight of a yellowish, half-liquid smoke trickling from the windows of the Countess's chamber. The pungent smell filling the hallway seemed to terrify the Countess's little dog, who goes unnamed in every published recounting. Let's call him Little Rex in this one. It sounds better than Old Pain-in-the-Ass, which surely he was called on occasion, being a version of Yorkie.

The maid burst into the room and saw the Countess on the floor in shocking dishabille. Not far from the bed was a heap of ashes. Only a pair of stockinged legs remained untouched. The maid remembered thinking how lovely those legs seemed; they were remarkable, considering. Maybe she even compared them to her own legs. It is not often that a maid gets to stare so at her mistress without fear of reprimand.

What a royal mess, the maid might have thought. *Come on, Rex,* she might have exhorted, *you're no help at all.* But she was still just a maid, and it was not really her business to exhort. Besides, whose cold tongue was lapping the Countess's face when all Hell broke loose? Who tried to take on those earliest flames lick for determined lick? Maybe at that moment Pain-in-the-Ass is the name Rex knows the maid by. He might have stopped shaking in his tiny canine booties long enough to wonder *Who does she think she's talking to?* He'd mean the maid right then, not the Countess the night before in her insistent praying. Asking for too much one last time. In bed, wrapped up in herself, so self-consumed you know there'll be no more talking to her.

iii. What a Town, What a Woman, What a Time

In 1780 in Limerick, Ireland a boardinghouse keeper O'Neill is awakened out of the sleep of his life by a lodger who insists O'Neill follow him back to his room. From the doorway they stare together at the charred body of Mrs. Peacock, a roomer on the floor above, lying *flaming and red as copper* in the lodger's otherwise-dark chamber. By the glow of Mrs. Peacock they can just barely make out the hole she's burned through the ceiling.

As a boy out walking the streets at night, our lodger was already in the habit of looking up. The Big Dipper was a cinch. Then Cassiopeia, the Lady in the Chair. Every glittering jewel in Orion's Belt. But this gaping hole overhead in the shape of a woman prone, this dark smoldering, this anti-constellation surely must have startled him: a flimsier universe than he dreamed, and small enough to fall out the bottom of without warning.

On other nights he might have prayed for something close to this occurrence, lighted a galaxy of candles in the asking of some kind of demonstrable love into his life, but what exactly was he supposed to do now? An entire tavern's worth of stout and still Mrs. Peacock is nothing he ever could have imagined. The too many dim light-years she'd travelled to get here, maybe. Maybe he can imagine those.

Some older kids explained how the rock he'd found near the schoolyard was probably a meteorite, how it had come from a completely different world. Eventually he knew even better: it was a fragment of that other world itself, now insinuated smack in the middle of his. A survivor of the scariest falling dream in the firmament, where everything's always burning down and too quickly out. By the time he discovers that much, it's already cool, whole, strangely familiar in his hands.

• • •

Or:

O'Neill's Own Theory

There once was a woman so hot
that she turned flaming red quite a lot.
When her ardent desire
translated as fire
she shocked men more often than not.

iv. All That Represents Him

From his days of newspaper reporting, his many perfunctory appearances at inquests, Charles Dickens is familiar with the notion of SHC. It's not because he's getting paid by the word that he writes down every bit of hearsay. Instead, he's drawn like a moth; he's working up a theory of his own. Years later he'll be responsible for one of the grisliest deaths in English literature when the newspaperman cum novelist kills off the villainous Krook in *Bleak House*.

Guppy and Weevle enter Krook's house in a squalid alley with more than their usual trepidation. Guppy: *What's the matter with the cat? Look at her! Mad, I think. And no wonder, in this evil place.*

Was it Guppy who'd read that the Countess di Bandi's dog was found cowering, terrified sixteen years earlier, driven mad by the fetid ooze that once had been its attentive mistress? Someone can't stop himself from carrying on:

There is a smoldering suffocating vapor in the room, and a dark greasy coating on the walls and ceiling. The chairs and table, and the bottle so rarely absent from the table, all stand as usual. . . .

Here is a burnt patch of flooring . . . and here is—not the cinder of a small charred and broken log of wood sprinkled with white ashes, or is it coal? O Horror, he is here! and this from which we run away, striking out the light and overturning one another into the street, is all that represents him.

To be so reduced, so represented. Or to be Guppy, to be Weevle, Laurel & Hardying into the pre-vaudevillian alley, bowlers askew, with no piano on the loose, no block of ice melting away in the tongs. Nothing to make us laugh while they're fussing and fuming, picking themselves up and finally hightailing it out of there, leaving behind what passes for moral decay in their circumscribed world.

Even his most loyal readers found the mode of death so preposterous, so literally unbelievable, that an incensed Dickens railed in a Foreword to a later edition: *Call the death by any name . . . attribute it to whom you will, it is the same death eternally— inborn, inbred, engendered in the corrupt humors of the vicious body itself, and that only—Spontaneous Combustion, and none other of all the deaths that can be died.*

To be Dickens, cum moralist cum scientist, and so bloody sure. While he's setting the evil drunkard's fire in *Bleak House,* he's corresponding with physicist Faraday about the latter's article, *Chemistry of a Candle,* where the real scientist suggests that burning a candle is almost like breathing: *In every one of us there is a living process of combustion going on very similar to that of a candle. . . . That is not merely true in a poetical sense—the relation of the life of a man to a taper. . . .*

Alcohol and hot blood: a bad mix. A combustible psychic cocktail. Even today the newspapers are full of people who can't handle it: the tavern brawls, the old-fashioned crimes of passion or impatience. Some people seem to lose it altogether and are gone, smoke into the ozone. And Dickens knew what he knew. Turn the page and one more tinderbox of vicious chromosomes is about to blow sky-high.

There are other pages full of pathetic human incandescence: in Melville, in Zola, in Gogol. It's raining corrupt humors like cats and dogs. Then one too many nights of serious drinking, and when the smoke clears there's nobody home.

And Dickens near the end of his life, still drawn. This time he's a tourist in Italy, foregoing the watery city of Venice. Instead, he's actually climbing the warm slopes of Vesuvius. Even after reaching the volcano's lip he presses on, despite warnings from his guides. He's staring into the pulsing magma, his head shrouded in the toxic smoke, when he collapses. If not for the prompt action of the guides, he might have fallen completely into the fiery crater.

Dickens consumed, imagination on fire. Dickens more at home writing feverishly into the night, breathing heavily, candles burning on the desk until the room goes totally dark.

Not merely true in a poetical sense.

* * *

Curly: It's this fever, I tell ya. I'm boinin' up.
   (He opens his mouth and smoke streams out.)

Moe: Oh, wiseguy, eh? Get over here, Hothead. We got woik to do.
   (He grabs Curly by the ears, then recoils. Instantly his hands are on fire.)

Curly: Nyuk nyuk nyuk.

Moe: (waving his arms) Porcupine, quick! Blow me out!

Larry: OK, OK, just a minute! Simmer down. I gotta think of somethin' to wish for.

* * *

And this from which we run away.

v. Ladybug, Fly Away Home

When Rickey Pruitt burst into flames and burned to death in 1959, he was only four months old—hardly one of *the elderly, the invalids, the indigent, the alcoholics, the persons weary with years and lost dreams that are the most frequent victims,* as researcher Gaddis would have it. Rickey burned so quickly down the short length of his life the candle barely had a chance to catch its breath. In just a little over a single season of slobber and diapery sleep, Rickey's hardly a flicker in the dark. A puff of smoke, the kind you'd see from the fingertips of the magician at a kid's birthday party, and Rickey Pruitt's gone from his unscorched crib.

He wasn't old enough to scream out words like *fire* or *hot,* or any words at all, but he must have screamed, must have had a feeling: some hunger gone awfully wrong. And Rickey's mother, how could she have foreseen that afternoon? Stove: *no, don't touch.* Radiator: *no, don't touch.* Iron: *no, don't touch.* Good boy, Rickey, wiser than his months, those years he'll never crawl into. Farsighted Rickey, who cried himself awake more days than not, who cried himself asleep for the rest of his life.

Rickey's mother genuinely believed it was part of God's larger plan. Apparently He's still trafficking in fire and other people's sons. *Let's see . . . for one more sure-fire test of faith I'll cross the burning bush I used on Moses with that bit about Abraham's Isaac and see how it turns out this time. God. What won't I think of next?*

Better we should remember the primordial ooze: back there on the beach, fire preceded language. First the wordless drooling of the suddenly multi-celled. Then, inexplicably, fire. Then the spirited talking and singing around it until finally someone looks up out of the centuries and reminds us: something's the matter with the cat.

And wherever he is now, that two-bit magician is doing his last trick of the afternoon, before he gets his measly check. He'll show them how much he'd rather not be there. He's vanishing lighted cigarettes in front of a bunch of five-year-olds. Not the most appropriate magic, maybe, for such a birthday party. But even Mr. Old Testament God, with his arrogant sleight-of-hand, is not always suitable for children.

Now the birthday boy's wearing the requisite party hat. Someone's taking pictures of him poised over the cake with its smattering of candles. He's done this all before: it's so simple, a child. And so he makes a wish and blows them out. They flare back up out of their stubborn little lives mired in the icinged goo. The joke is on him, but he's still too young to get it. What happens to all his wishing now? He's mystified. He's crying. A second ago his family and friends were laughing, urging him to try again. Now they're not sure what to do.

vi. Trying to Make Light of It: An Interlude

Every day someone crawls out of his ocean of sleep
and takes those first tottering steps on the planet again
he's playing with real fire.
He's courting a fever of epic proportions
until the mercury bubbles, explodes out the top of the throbbing
cartoon thermometer. And then some clown with a bucket
rides up on a bicycle and hits him full in the face
with a splash of confetti and streamers. Yeah,
that's about as funny as a firetruck or a funeral.

vii. Billy and the Saints

In the same year Rickey Pruitt flickered out and The Fleetwoods whispered *Come Softly to Me,* Billy Peterson was the hottest case of SHC on record. He was found smoldering in his Impala, not unlike a lot of young men in 1959. The radio, still tuned to his favorite station, pounding out its rock 'n' roll.

He'd dressed in jeans and a starched white T before heading into his Saturday night. Not only were his clothes unsinged, but every hair stuck up intact through his charred-to-the-third-degree flesh. Rather like the victims of atomic flash-and-burn, this whiff of Hiroshima come to the outskirts of Detroit. Reportedly his groin was *burned to a crisp,* and he's not merely dreaming his usual back-seat dream this time. There's nothing nearly metaphorical enough about a hurt as low-down deep as that.

This is 1959. Sputnik's a dizzy two years old. The Five Stars' *Atom Bomb Baby* still gets a lot of play: *She's just the way I want her to be / A million times hotter than TNT.* . . . A particularly 1950s twist on the old popular song convention of equating sexuality with heat. An earlier generation scorched the dance floors coast-to-coast to The Nighthawk Orchestra's *Flaming Mamie.* That was 1926, when atoms were still oblique: benevolent and wise. Before the Fall from Atomic Grace, before the story of Atom & Evil.

The car's in good shape, its full tank of gas untouched. The hula girl dangling from the rear-view mirror is completely herself in this suddenly tropical December. But the melted plastic on the dash is another story, all that's left of Billy's religious statues and what they stood for: Billy's devotion, his faith in them to see him through. That's a lot of pressure, if you're the sainted kind. You never get only your praises sung. You have to take the heat when one more lowly mortal feels he can't, and lets you know it. It's hard to make out specifics in this sticky residue of saints. But there's no doubting Billy Peterson tonight.

This can't be a Fire from Heaven any more than *Little Boy* was, dropped nose-first out of the *Enola Gay.* Although that's exactly how an American priest, visiting near Hiroshima at the time, actually chose to describe what he witnessed.

Let's blast back to another Golden Oldie, circa 1950: Lowell Blanchard and The Valley Trio's *Jesus Hits Like an Atom Bomb,* a metaphor either cruel or incredibly naive, depending on where you put most of your faith: tenor, or flashy vehicle.

OK. It's 1959 again. Barbie's just been launched, virginal and cool, into the powderkeg world. Jack Lemmon and Tony Curtis are hot-footing it to Miami, disguised as members of an all-girl band. There are more serious notes: Holly, Valens, and The Bopper have gone irretrievably down in Clear Lake, Iowa. And Billy Peterson's just gone up. He's alone at the top of the baffled doctors' charts. This is the year of being assured we've just crossed over into *The Twilight Zone.*

We'll be rockin' through the rest of '59, playin' the best of '59. Right now it's The Crests comin' at ya with Sixteen Candles. *Can ya handle Anka's* Lonely Boy *after that? I'll take the next caller and we'll dedicate a song, send it out with some tender devotion to whosoever in the wide wide world you choose to favor with the news: you're drownin' in that cool cool* Sea of Love.

Finally, some positive ID's: Christopher, patron saint of travellers. Jude, patron saint of hopeless causes. The Virgin Mary, the worse for wear, reduced but still haloed in streetlight. Don't forget the blonde goddess Marilyn, hilariously down-to-earth as Sugar Kane in Wilder's *Some Like It Hot.*

Mother and Bombshell of us all.

Atom Bomb Baby, boy, she can start / One of those chain reactions in my heart.

The Fire from Whatever-Isn't-Heaven.

Police report no signs of a struggle.

I'm droppin' the needle into the groove again and again for you. Ya know what they say is true: rock 'n' roll will never die—as long as the Devil favors somethin' he can dance to.

And atoms will forever be our reliable sidekicks, our invisible, warm-hearted friends. Let us pray:

So Billy Peterson, if you're listening, this one's going out to you with a whole lotta love from Brenda, who says she's sorry about the other guys, but she just wanted some reaction. Who says her heart will always be on fire for only you.

viii. His Side of the Story

Aura Troyer was walking his broom down the last few stairs to the basement after another night of sweeping the bank where he worked as *the best damn janitor in the state of Illinois*. He had that printed on a thousand business cards he'd sent away for in the mail, if anyone would ask. For a minute it was more than an honest living, this way he'd found to make ends almost meet. What lay ahead he couldn't say from one day to the next. But whatever he'd find there, he'd get it straightened out. He'd try to make it shine.

One more night in the dustbin. One more night down the drain. One more bucket of industrial cleaner, the extra strength needed for the toughest job: wiping out those dreams of what life must be like a floor or two above him. Aura Troyer, humming in the basement, giving it the once-over before locking up. Before throwing himself into the long walk home.

A man whose life was cleanliness and order, everything in its place. It must have hurt him most of all, insult strewn on top of injury: this raging out of control. He was one of the few who lived long enough to say anything for the record: *it happened all of a sudden*. Nothing terribly profound, but at least it's neat and clean. What else would we have him say from his ineffable side of the story?

He must have meant the flames themselves spreading out from somewhere deep inside him—not the burning he managed so well most days to live with, scouring the ironic premises for loose change, an occasional stray dollar falling his way, the paycheck that barely covered him alone in his bed at night. The blaze always starts in closed, cramped quarters: the brain, the heart, the small intestine. Some snippet of nerve in the intricate network of feeling. Miraculous, how many people keep it so contained: an almost bearable heat in the boiler room that sustains them. The heart, a furnace in what amounts to a closet of ammonia, brushes, and mops. And the pain rings the nerves in the dead of night like a dire long-distance call. It sails through the blood until it chokes on itself, a thousand paper boats on fire. And when the furnace finally blows there's no easy escape, no sure way of climbing out alive.

All of a sudden should be reserved for last call at the neighborhood tavern, for spontaneous murder or love. The strongest craving for whatever sweets. As if we'd be not nearly as much to blame as we are when anything in our lives goes bad more gradually, iota by crucial iota, and we can see it turning. There's no excuse for the milk in its carton, where the reasonable limit of our expectations was so clearly stamped, gone too sour to swallow.

It happened all of a sudden . . . but even the Wicked Witch of the West put fire in the form of a question, no matter how rhetorical, to the Scarecrow. He had a minute to reckon his fear, put his strawman affairs in order. He could see it coming, spelled out at the business end of the broom. Would that some Dorothy were always around, doing some quick thinking for us. It's true: usually the answer to fire like that is water. But Aura Troyer knows his trade, those conflagrations water won't put out. Our only hope: some last-ditch chemicals the brain thinks up, manufactures on a frenzied moment's notice.

All his panicky brain can shake loose: one of those *Mommy Mommy* sick jokes making the rounds at the time:

> *Kid:* Mommy! Mommy! Daddy's on fire!
> *Mother:* Quick! The marshmallows!

If Aura Troyer had lived to offer a leisurely telling of his story, he'd be pushing a more sanitized version. There'd be no noxious odor emanating from the basement, ever. No scorch marks on the white tile floor. He'd wipe out his own ending, the pitiful condition he was found in. Why run the risk of spilling over into sentimentality—something there's no easy cleaning up after? Take it from the best damn janitor in Illinois.

What remains: the bare bones of the story. Aura Troyer, indistinguishable from his broom. So much straw for the fire.

ix. Long Day at the Beach

The most thoroughly investigated instance: Mary Reeser, St. Petersburg, Florida, who burned while she sat in her favorite easy chair. Dozens of official, gruesome photographs: charred liver fused to a piece of backbone, skull shrunk to baseball size, a foot encased in a black satin slipper. The rest is a perfect circle of ash. Outside of that, the pristine draperies. Piles of newspapers and magazines that resisted the notion of flames.

At first Dr. Wilton Krogman, forensic fire-death specialist, a master of what's burned past any recognition, was confused: *I cannot conceive of such complete cremation without more burning of the apartment itself. In fact the apartment and everything in it should have been consumed. Never have I seen a human skull shrunk by intense heat. The opposite has always been true. . . . As I review it, the short hairs on my neck bristle with vague fear. Were I living in the Middle Ages, I'd mutter something about Black Magic.*

But not for long. These are not the hocus-pocus Middle Ages, and experts are obliged to enunciate expertly. Let there be no confusion: Krogman finally decided that Mary Reeser had been taken from her room, murdered and burned elsewhere, and then returned to her apartment by the killer, who *ingeniously supplied the other touches:* the exacting four-foot circle of ash, the soot on the walls, the doorknob still hot enough to blister the worried landlady's hand. And the oppressive swelter in the room, even hours later.

The perfect cover for the perfect crime: spontaneous human combustion. No noisy struggle. No smoking gun. No fingerprints anyone can hope to dust for.

Krogman knows his Dickens, or at least the precious little he's found references to in the literature of forensics and fire. He's made it his business, this burning cadavers every way that's humanly possible in his research lab at Penn. He's taking on the Siamese twins of mysteries: need and desperation, joined at the hip: how molecules of flesh and fire work out their fragile, short-lived symbiosis.

So round up the usual suspects: the Ph.D.'s in English.

The local paper challenged readers to concoct their own explanations. From Sarasota to Clearwater they came pouring in: careless smoking, suicide by gasoline, grease fire, faulty wiring. The hazards of synthetic fabrics, flying saucers, sympathetic magic. Honorable Mention, Most Sinister Originality: Mary as unwitting victim of government testing, a secret atomic pill exchanged for her nightly dose of Seconal. But at the last, an unsigned postcard addressed to *Cheif of Detectiffs*, claiming: *A ball of fire came through the window and hit her. I seen it happen.* And suddenly it's no contest.

Hard to believe it can really be that simple: the way the sun can come in through the window and hit us all wrong, some morning in the middle of a week already gone awry. How we might feel the heat at the base of the spine, the back of the neck, a stinging in the eyes and we're sweating it out again: a pile of flimsy emotional kindling wrapped in a nightshirt. It's a two-alarm morning at least. No wonder some people crash and burn. The only mystery is how anyone gets up at all and walks away from the infernal snap and crackle as the bedframe splinters and collapses and the cotton batting of one more dream is immolated in a flash, a matchtip's worth of sunrise.

In Florida, like so many places where people search out reasons for the unbearable, there's a popular theory: it's not the heat, it's the humidity.

Krogman knows a human being is virtually a sack of mostly salty water, a quintessence that leaks out gradually over a lifetime in the sweating, the bleeding, the pissing, the coming, and the crying. And often he's amazed that fire ever stands a chance, going up against an arsenal like that.

Consider the lightning playing in the sky over western Florida that night. Heat lightning, so bright in its intermittent flashes that the few stars otherwise visible disappeared. And down on the beach—where the ocean laps at the ankles of whoever's there right now, thinking about walking out into it, back into the primal water—someone's looking up. Because so much of what passes for this life on dry land falls short of that eons-old promise, its blazing assurance lighting up the dark.

The stars were shimmering, absolute facts before astronomers named them. Before anyone made any connections between them, drew those imaginary lines that gave them their parts in a larger story. And it's true: by the time they shed their modicum of light on the likes of us, often they've already burned down to the last wisp of gases. They're over, and out. Off the aberrational air for good.

Just ask our keen-eyed, anonymous confidant down there at the water's edge. Ask if seeing really is believing, for surely this desperate person needs some story to swear by. This electrifying night it's hard to make out details clearly through the clouds, the lightning, the hazy salt air. That might be a faint Aquarius, the Water Carrier. And that's conceivably a piece of the Little Dipper. What's left irrefutable overhead tonight is the unlikely story to end all unlikely stories: a brilliant rendition of the Lady in the Chair. She's restored to her former glory from somewhere nearly beyond recognition, her eyes shining and her quiet life wholly explicable again.

That's the good news. And although it travels relatively fast, it always has such a long way to go.

And the bad news no one's in a hurry for is pulling on its pants in our dark bedroom, cigarette glowing in its enormous mouth. Any minute it'll be sauntering through the living room in our slippers on its way to the kitchen, looking for something else to eat.

x. Where There's Smoke

And where there's fire you often find someone staring
into the red-hot, flickering heart of the matter,
losing himself in it for moments or days
or years at a time. Joining that enormous circle
of everyone who's ever gathered near a fire
looking for something to say, another log to throw on,
some version of a story called We Are All In This Together,
to our varying degrees. Spreading it by word of mouth,
by firelight, through the haunted woods of history.
That animal bellying out of the water back there
where this whole shebang began really started something:
communion with its fiercely elemental opposite. And now
around all kinds of fires the same inevitable stories
break out: we're offering up small pieces of ourselves
disguised as someone else. We're burning effigies.

If we could somehow rise above it, wrapped up
in a warm blanket of air, and look down on the planet tonight,
we'd see thousands of tiny telltale fires.
The whole world's spinning stories like there's no tomorrow.
There are people who can't wait for the next one
and people who can't sleep, who know too many already.
And people you wouldn't believe who'll sleep much better
for having faced down the fire, sticking it out
until the end, until it's immutably in their hair,
in their reddened eyes, and whatever they're wearing
reeks of it forever. And still they're not quite overcome.
They walk away ashen and suddenly cold, but they're alive.

Sure, we'd each rather be the mysterious figure
King Nebuchadnezzar couldn't believe in the fiery furnace,
shoulder to shoulder with Shadrach, Meshach, and Abednego.

Swelling the ranks of those who will not burn up, who refuse
on principle, even in the midst of Babylon's brightest fire.
That kind of inextinguishable faith, their way
of fighting fire with fire. We're stuck blowing on the ashes
of vague hope, looking for even the smallest spark.

It's hard to know when to quit. There's always one more story
that seemed like such a good idea at the time.
There used to be days we burned with good ideas too.
Our faces glowed on those occasions we couldn't believe
how much there still was to look forward to:
cars that ran, books we wanted to read,
a flavor of ice cream we hadn't tried and the rest
of the hundred and one known positions. These days
we know the tissue-thin stuff we're made of, and we're afraid
we'd never pass even a routine inspection. We're mostly living
breathing hazards: at least one strand of nerve hanging loose
somewhere we'd never think to look. We can check the stove
as often as we'd like, make sure the ashtray's cold
before talking ourselves out the door.
But right now there's a neuron deliriously firing,
playing hell with that ticklish mix of chemicals and spit
that holds us together. And let's be honest: we come apart
so easily, so often without warning or alarm.

At our best, walking down the street in broad daylight
there might even be a piece of a song
we feel *this* close to bursting into, but we don't.
Because what if the words don't come? It could be tears
or flame instead, a flash of the old consuming passion,
then a sigh, the shortest story of all:
one last lick of smoke taking the air, leaving everything
inviolate for miles around, as if nothing so unbelievable,
so spontaneously human, ever could have happened here.

• • •

They've finally caught up with that neighborhood kid.
They've found him with a magnifying glass in his hand,
bending over a crack in the sidewalk loaded with ants.
He's just learning how small this inflammatory world can be,
how to make his squeamish way in it.
How much longer did you think he'd remain
in the dark? Let's give him the benefit of our doubt:
say he's simply magnifying everything he can think of
until it seems so much larger than life.
That it's an accident he's gathering any light he can find
and reducing it to this white-hot, concentrated point.
That he has no idea what's about to happen.
Let's pretend his heart's too naive to master
the simple art of deflection. Yes, there's fire burning
behind his eyes already, but surely there's no crime in that.
He's trying to keep it under control, but that's hard
when you're a kid in the summer with the rest of your life
like a fuse lit in the heat of some unforeseen moment
inconceivable years down the road
and burning back to somewhere you're headed for right now,
towards the repercussive powders packed tightly inside you.

If they were to bring him in for questioning today,
sit him under the hot interrogation lights
while they gave him the third degree, he'd have no idea
what they wanted. The way he sees it, everyone else
has a lot of explaining to do.
He's nothing more than the flimsiest material
witness wherever he goes, released forever
on the reckless strength of his own recognizance.

IV. In the Boondocks of What's Possible

Just imegine your "ectospasm" running around William and Nilliam among the unlimitless etha—golla, it's imbillivibil.

—Krazy Kat, as told to George Herriman

Why Certain Poets Have No Business at the Track

for Pete G.

This afternoon the grandstand's full of greenhorns betting horses
by the ring of their names in the suddenly rarefied racetrack air.
For the poets, the morning line's always good enough
and now when the honest work should begin, they have nothing to do
with the latest numbers posted on the tote. They've got one system
down so cold it never wavers, splitting hairs of assonance
between *Liar's Dice* and *Will-o'-the-Wisp*. They altogether rule out
Risky Business. Who's a mudder, who's a step away from glue, who's
the jockey riding a streak? The poets can't be bothered. Already
they have an image of themselves at home in their own bright silks,
worrying a possible line break instead of the hairline fracture
doctored moments before *Sky's the Limit* falls into the gate.
It won't be anything metaphorical when the 4-horse pulls up lame.

The poets have arrived at a consensus, and they're off
racing to the last-minute window, laying their wrong money down.
It's a good thing they've come with their usual little to lose.
That's why, if Wordsworth were alive, he'd be much better off
somewhere in Vegas at baccarat, or better yet in the middle of
a backroom poker game, intoning some romantic variation
on the predictable *shut up and deal*. At least he'd have some idea
he's in way over his head, should go back to wandering lonely.
It's a good thing Mr. Eliot and his buddies stayed mostly home.

The track exudes an easy sucker's ambiance, too much temptation
to say to a certain poet's self: *through these binoculars I can see
the world in microcosm.* They always get it that exactly

backwards, staring the wrong way through the glass, already
making everything in sight inconsequentially small.
And they'll go home, poorer but immeasurably wiser, and write poems
and place them in the country's most courageous magazines
where people brave enough to really read those kinds of things
will show them to meeker associates who will marvel at the pomp
and unlikely circumstance, the calculated risk of a little local color.
And the folks worlds away from those things, who wouldn't find a copy
of *Green Banana Street Review* at their newsstand on a bet,
have no idea what they're missing. Yet they seem so unreasonably happy

as long as the new day's Racing Form is there, promising nothing but
what matters in every line, what's actually worth remembering
past the morning coffee, through the snarl of traffic on the way
to another chance at their glorious day in the sun. And God,
as the racetrack faithful enter their scratches, how they hope
the poets will stay home today. Or let them go fishing,
raise their eloquent children, or tour a few ruins
of ancient cities they can found sonnet sequences on.
A patient jock riding a quick horse is all good railbirds are asking.
The perfect alliance of form and content,
as that Frankie Villon would say to Not-So-Fast Eddie Poe
and they'd both laugh, were they not in their cups,
the odds of them sobering up in time to collect on their hunches
going off at an outrageous 100-1.

The Humming

When my nerves declare themselves
just that much more bad wiring in the thin walls
of my life, and now I'm an accident
or a miracle waiting to happen, depending
on who's making the inspection,
on nights like this too long and quiet for words
I can still hear Debbie Fuller humming at her desk,
her pencil hovering above a blank map of the world
in 4th-grade geography, and I'm leaning over again
trying to see where she's put the Mediterranean.
So much seemed to be riding on it, but it was only
a test, no different from hundreds we'd face down
through the years. Yet somewhere she'd learned early
how the notion of faith can be undone in quiet rooms,
an old sweater that frays, unravels, comes apart
in your sweaty hands. That's when we need to hear the motor
running under the hood of our best intentions: the clean,
fast getaway. Some audible surge of courage to steer by.

There are nights we could almost believe it's genuinely
song, the only music left when the day's drained out its due.
Anything but our own anxious breathing rearranged
because out of nowhere there's a pulse along the tongue,
inside the eyeteeth, a beating against the roof
of the mouth and we press our lips this tightly together:
the heart's *that* close to going out.

It's the scat of worriers and dreamers, the ones without
any hope they can truly put into words.
Right now it's hard to tell one from the other.

This is where humming gets us every time:
until what's going to happen sooner or later actually
happens, there's not another blessed thing to do.
Listen. There's a lot of bucking up
in the air tonight. The whole world's one concerted hum.
The typewriter's humming a long time between lines.
The furnace trembles and sighs, but mostly
there's humming through the vents. It's never easy
past midnight when the radio's humming its version of
white noise where the doo-wop station faded too fast,
and block after city block, amazingly, every streetlight
is humming for once, holding off its calculated share
of the dark. Along miles of power lines
countless words are reduced to split-seconds of humming
strung out, person-to-person, in all directions
until those tiny bones in the inner ear of whoever
may be listening are stirred, start humming mightily
themselves, and someone's finally got a good connection.

Something high-pitched from the stars is being recorded
on sensitive machinery, some signal that might mean
months or years of translation. But for now it comes through
distinctly as humming, even scientists recognize that much.
And there's something in the way a planet hums
its way around the sun, one huge blur of worry or wishing
locked in endless orbit around what it's drawn to, irresistibly,
millions of miles deep in its galaxy. And there are nights
we've known that kind of gravity, felt it that strongly
in the solar plexus or at least in the heels of our boots.

Right this minute there's a woman in a parked car
humming around a man, and he's humming back,
if only she could hear him, for all he's worth tonight.
They're so wide awake they can't be dreaming,

and what other choice do they finally have
with something humming that deep in the blood?
While the car engine's humming, the defroster's humming,
and now they've kicked open the glove compartment
and street maps are unfolding all over the place.
There must be close to a dozen cities at their feet, but already
that's yesterday's itinerary. They still have no idea,
in these new latitudes of humming, where they go from here.

And I bet Debbie Fuller's humming, wherever she is,
like there's no tomorrow. As if she knows her life
is being ransacked again for one more of its small, pure lessons.
She may not realize that half a mile from where I'm still awake
the Mississippi's humming south in its long bed,
but I bet she could pick out the Mississippi, still knows France
when she sees it, and would never confuse St. Louis for Paris
or put either on the wrong side of whatever river.
She's up another night with dreams that just won't quit:
she's taking a test for us all in a subject
she can barely imagine while we crowd in tightly around her,
hopelessly drawn to her humming.

She's losing sleep over us years later still trying
to get any grip on the complex geography of the heart,
trying to get some part of it down, legibly,
unmistakably, whatever we can make of it just now.
Before we have to let go of our pencils again and hope
that miraculously from somewhere in the back of the room,
from out of the almost unearthly quiet,
some anthem we never learned words to will work
its accidental magic, will hum us, lift us entirely
out of one more bewildering day in the world
we'd have to give ourselves, were it only up to us,
no small amount of credit for signing our right names to.

Goodbye Note to Debbie Fuller: Pass It On

Whoever this Debbie Fuller is in your poems, she ought to be collecting royalties.

—a loyal reader

When we passed those notes to each other and laughed
behind Miss Jago's back in Hamilton School, we were flirting
with real danger. The secret insults and atonement
that passed for our friendship seemed effortless in cursive,
too easily could have become a part of our Permanent Record.
Those days we got away with more than we ever imagined,
so many ways of saying I'm sorry again, I won't do it
anymore, and I promise not to get you
into trouble from now on. As if we could help ourselves.

If I've named names under pressure in my life since then
in the late-night interrogation rooms of the heart,
if I've had to write out one more doctored confession,
give up on maintaining my innocence one more night
and your name is the one I keep coming back to,
I'll admit it: you're the alibi I've needed, the only one
who can place me miles and years away from the dried blood,
the chalked outline of childhood on the sidewalk. Otherwise
I'm looking at some serious hard time, and you know
I'll be taking you with me.

Say I fell hard for those dirty blonde bangs, those doleful eyes,
those corduroy skirts and OK, finally, even the way you moved
to Basking Ridge, New Jersey that December of '65
without breathing a word to anyone, not even to me
in the holiday assembly when I was the top of the wobbling

human Christmas tree and you placed that cardboard star on my head
with a kiss we never practiced in rehearsal.
How could you know what you were lighting up forever,
improvising one last piece of business that was nowhere
in the script? Maybe no one told you either,
or you didn't know how to say it. Maybe that day was
your rendition of uncanny grace under pressure.
I was ten and thought I knew everything
I could possibly want for Christmas for the rest of my life.

I wanted you earlier in the alphabet, or taller, depending
on any given day's meticulous instructions for lining up
on our way to whatever came next. My faintest hope was always
rained-out gym, huddled inside, boy-girl-boy-
girl for almost an hour, no questions asked. God, I wanted you
to realize how much it mattered too. Those were the days
before love knew its own name, almost before hormones
in their nervous skirmishes at the borders of wherever we were.

I don't know why, after so many years of everything
I've put you through in words—silent partner
in a thousand schemes, or worse, my unwitting accomplice—
you still keep coming back to me. As if it's been in your power
to refuse, as if you've had anything to say. I'll confess again:
I've used you, but I guess I'd like to think I haven't
used you up completely. So here's my promise at long last:
you won't have to get dressed on short notice, hurry out of a house
full of people who love you more for whatever you've become.
No more questions of *what do I wear* in this poem, *what
can he possibly want from me now?* I'll leave you alone
to look me up in your own quiet version of time.

And people who insist on reading this before it gets to you
can sigh and shake their heads if they want to, as long

as they keep it moving while the world drones on
through its baffling arithmetic, geography without end,
through its far-flung chalky sense of history
while the radiators hiss and the clock lops off another minute
you're too far away to whisper all this in your ear.
As long as they know this one's for Debbie Fuller,
for old times' sake, for all the good it does,
from the kid still making any promise he can get away with:
it won't happen again, I swear,
or your name's not Debbie Fuller. Debbie Fuller,
it won't ever happen again.

Carnival Heaven

Every once in a while there's some small-town preacher out to save our sorry souls by bringing God to the carnival.

—Sammy the Flash, pitchman

It was an idea that must have looked good on paper: God
in his ballyhooed wisdom, toned down for the occasion, turned loose
on the midway to talk the gentle talk, to shine his just and merciful light
in ways no bought-off local flatfoot ever could.

But God's not sure why he really had to be booked into Keokuk, Iowa,
this carnival lot a far cry from any heyday version of Gomorrah.
Nevertheless, when God deigns to get involved in the mortal thick of things,
wherever, he can't help calling attention to himself. You do that
if you're God. He knows the psychology of the masses, how to work a crowd
for its undying love and walk-around money. Each time he says Step Right Up
and they do, he can barely contain himself. He can't believe the suckers
just asking for it, the old two-bit theatrics: a little flash, another dab
of hubba-hubba. Ask Adam and Eve, or Moses. Ask Father Abraham.
Ask the roofer who's blowing off a whole day's wages right now
tossing those gigantic rings at the impossible color TV. He'll get his
Better Luck Next Time. Ask any of God's incredulous children:
there's one born every minute. And knowing everything he knows,
God's got to like his chances tonight.

Historically, the power of God's love is everywhere, but here
it's mostly lost in the crowd. It's lost on the guy who guesses weights.
He can't even begin to fathom God, so God's back every few minutes
shaking his head *no* again, picking out another of those plastic squirting gags:
prize carnations, bow ties, cameras, pinkie rings. God knows craftsmanship
when he sees it. He doesn't miss a trick.

It's lost on the fortuneteller, who should have seen this coming.
Her tent's as empty as Monday church. God's giving away the future
in small talk, making it up as he goes along. The knife-thrower's daughter
spinning on her Wheel of Death doesn't want to hear it. It's lost
on the sword-swallower, who believes only in his living by the sword.

And it's lost in The Museum of Nature's Mistakes. God's making
his paltry amends, laying hands all over The Fish Boy and his brother
The Spider King. They're bathed in the half-hearted light of his countenance.
They'll wake up tomorrow, by the uncalled-for grace of God irretrievably whole,
and walk off the lot, off display forever into the garish, overblown world
of corporations, traffic, personal checks, and exquisite furniture showrooms.

But there's no love lost among the dancers in Amber's G-String Revue,
where right now God's sitting in his front-row seat, throwing dollar bills
furiously onto the stage. Last night God looked down from a long way off
and still he saw that it was good.

Clearly the reverend's plan isn't working. God's
got a plan or two of his own, now that he's actually come
to feel oddly at home, expansive in this summer night on the planet
amid mosquitoes and sweat, diesel engines humming, all the sticky hoopla
this far away from Heaven. He's a natural in neon, God
and his sudden entourage elbowing past the wide-eyed rubes everywhere
and laying their sure-fire money down. There's no flim-flam on Earth
he hasn't already considered. He knows his way around the rackets
like the pea understands its complicity, its own trinity of shells.

He rolls up his sleeves, runs his fingers through his James Dean hair
and sledges the block to the top of the High Striker again. The bell
sounds like crazy and the local high school girls whisper among themselves,
sighing wistfully. If only God had thought of the convertible tonight,
he could surely work a few of his strange and mysterious ways.

And while his angels seem content to preen and coo on the Ferris Wheel,
God's racking up Skee-Ball points with a vengeance,
he's shooting the eyes out of Ducks-on-a-Pond,
he's piling up cartons of cigarettes with his uncanny knack at The Razzle.
He's the Winner Every Time operators hate to see coming
in his ridiculous souvenir straw hat, carrying a raft of animals
in colors Noah never dreamed of.

Until he arrives at the booth where the Three Milk Bottles have stood
through the carnival ages. And although he's exerting his considerable might,
a full hour later he's still trying to knock them over
with a single, all-powerful throw. He's calling up some of that famous
Old Testament anger. He's sending for more bratwurst, popcorn and Sno-Cones,
more Biggest-Man-Alive cups of ice-cold beer. He's working a Lucky
loose from its pack and getting a little obnoxiously self-righteous,
pointing to the moon, the stars, every dazzling woman in the blurry firmament
and shouting *I came up with this* and *I made that.*
It's quickly turning into
the longest night in Creation. God's getting the slightest bit sick
to his stomach. And if he's really supposed to be everywhere at once,
imagine how the night's gone sour, turned ugly without warning
in Dubuque, Tuscaloosa, Moline, Sandusky. In towns all over New Jersey
and a thousand other stops on the circuit of the mostly civilized world.

God can feel the entire planet spinning, and even now the Devil's
grinning in his trailer, doing what he does best: licking his thin lips,
adding up the take. He's sending God a special tray of Vienna Red Hots
with everything. With his obsequious compliments. And what the hell:
a VIP pass good for all the ride time he's God enough to handle
on this thing God never thought of and called the Tilt-a-Whirl.

In Case of Rapture

Warning: in case of Rapture, this car will be unmanned.

— bumper sticker

And with my usual brand of luck I'll be in the car
right behind, cursing, leaning on the horn, as always
getting nowhere fast. And this time the old man
so ubiquitous in his homburg will stop completely,
roll down the window, and slowly bail out of his Chevrolet
to join hands with a woman already rising above the corner bakery.
Say the word and there goes the entire fish-fry contingent
from the local Kingdom Hall, called home somewhere between grace
and potato salad until the sky's so full of old-time religion
broad daylight's common sense is utterly eclipsed.
In case of Rapture, I'll try not to stare. Clearly
these people can't help the way they suddenly appear.
Besides, looking directly at a spectacle like that
could mean going blind. These things always seem to happen
on the road to somewhere. Saul and his Damascus. Me and my A&P.

No wonder there's no shortage of preachers when you're driving,
more than ever occur to you on the radio at home.
Minutes from my nightcap at the Idle Hour I'm blessed:
we'll float upward just like helium balloons is the way
this gospel man guarantees me. The balloon's his idea
of a metaphor, but not the being lifted. That's belief itself,
more for what it is than what it's like: to be that literally
exalted, that assuredly lighthearted.
To have that much faith in the promise of thin air.

It isn't long before I'm leaning on the jukebox
and laughing it up with the regulars, telling them exactly
how I heard it, word for unbelievable word.
The guy shooting pool knows better, says he's here to testify:
no matter how many can't-miss shots he still has in him,
he's learned to count only on the money in his pocket right now,
believes even if the Rapture comes tonight, tomorrow's likely
to be just another day on the planet.
And after all, he's the man of old-fashioned science,
the professor of gravity. He figures what rises
has to fall sometime: the lazy fly to right,
whole civilizations, the balloon some kid attaches a note to
before she lets go, fully expecting it one day to come down
anywhere but in her own backyard. He chalks it up
to history, to how he's seen it happen so often
to even the slightest hope, genuine faith's fainter sister.

If he's turning a little too solemn, blame the serious drinking,
a lot of nights mostly like this one, waiting
for a stiff wind the spirit could positively soar in,
not so much like a bird or a bright-colored leaf or a kite
or a lighter-than-air balloon. Surely there is no comparison,
no way of saying what it's like. Metaphor is an assurance
we'll know something when we finally feel it,
but we could wait a lifetime for wind strong enough
to get that completely carried away.

                           •   •   •

For now it's clear skies. Not a soul in sight.
There's no illumination beyond the ordinary
light from stars that have made it this far through the dark,
not another car on the road. Maybe the Rapture's come

and gone while the good people lay home in their beds,
manning their dreams until they were roused way out of them.
Maybe they're already rising to some dimly imagined occasion,
and we who remain behind are finally left alone
to our own God-forsaken devices, wearing the conspicuous smiles
of the damned, the ones so far removed from any saving grace
that we might yet make a kingdom of it
here, in the rest of the only lives we can swear to.

I'd really like to leave it at that. I've got a cold six
back in the icebox tonight, just in case of Rapture.
In case I feel the need to stay up late celebrating, not believing
I'd ever live out my days like the way-too-faithful,
ever carelessly mistake whatever isn't hell
for part of heaven: a glass of house brand whiskey,
a postcard in the mailbox, a car noise I can actually make
my doubting mechanic hear. But there have been nights so long
the heart sputters, running on empty promises again,
and I've said whatever I've had to say, talking it up
on the chance I'd somehow rise above those nights, radiant, once
and for all. Be plucked from behind the sweaty wheel
of too many harrowing miles in a row. Be lifted clean away.

Driving home this far past midnight I'm not above conceding
there may be some goings-on in the boondocks of what's possible
that pass for the miraculous, no matter how inflated,
things that happen so far beyond words
there'd be simply no telling. Try
and you could end up looking wildly for all the world
like someone you'd never believe, even at high noon
with you and your down-to-earth frustration right behind him,
watching him with your own eyes, undeniably floating
out of your life. And you'd have to insist it's nothing
you ever expected, not on those days you need to get through

in a hurry. Not when horns are blaring for miles
because suddenly you're the one inexplicably stalling,
holding everything up. It's your face, frantic, looking back
in the rear-view mirror. But no one else has any idea
what's next, exactly where you're supposed to go from here.

A Long Way from the Starlight

*Under hypnosis, UFO abductees often are able to recall the unsettling events that occurred on board
the craft during a period of what's usually no more than a few hours they cannot account for in their
waking lives. This aspect of the phenomenon is known as* Missing Time.

—from a symposium, "UFOs in the '90s"

When it came to the Starlight Drive-In, everyone I knew
was willing to go to extremes: hunkering down in the back seat,
laying low, packed together in the dark of someone's trunk. We thought
so little of using up our lives, a couple of hours at a time,
in the washed-out glow of the Starlight
where feature after cheesy feature reeled off its bargain basement share
of the only intelligent life in the universe we wanted in on: *Teenagers
from Space. Invaders from Mars. Catwomen of the Moon.*

And like it or not, I remember them all without even trying.
Whatever I might have been thinking at the time, it turns out
that most things aren't nearly forgettable enough:
not the obligatory scientist's earnest and beautiful daughter
falling one more time for the cub reporter who can't believe his luck.
Not the sad, radiated creature growing to fifty times its natural size.
Not any hapless alien a long way from home who means us
no harm. Not any who does. Not another histrionic question mark
when we all finally make it to *The End?* Not the most inept *Attack of . . .*
nor the dumbest *Brain That. . . .* Not the smallest *Thing*, that misguided
piece of 1950s bad advice, *Watch the skies.* As if some grade-B
human vigilance might somehow be enough to guarantee
that whatever happened there that night surely would never happen again.

And I wish I could be one of those people who never stopped watching
but remember only under hypnosis what they saw, taking themselves seriously
back to that time they can't fathom any other way, to a place
where everything's strangely in focus for once, made up
of amazing circumstances that never occur to them otherwise: space ships,
examination tables, telepathy in the nude, vaguely biological
experimentation. Now they're lying down again, counting backwards
from 10, and in their deepest artificial sleep they can't stop
dreaming up story after story they've been chosen to star in.
They're covering that stretch of road again between where they were picked up
and where they were inevitably let down. Between the car stalling out
and the engine running again like a dream where nothing ever really came off
between the swagger at midnight and the cold sweat at 2 AM.
These days they pour their whole lives into filling the hole
in a day they didn't even know was there.
And I don't know where they find that kind of time.

Something like that should be harder to forget, especially in a world
so full of smaller oddball wonders it's impossible to stop recollecting:
the light in the attic of a childhood that went out
with no warning, freezing you in the sudden dark. Daydreaming through
Debbie Fuller's Brownie uniform while she carried on nobly
with a bad day's Show-and-Tell. How the school nurse smiled and swore
this would be the last shot of anything you'd ever need.
The capital of Wyoming, maps made out of soap, Avogadro's Number,
the Pythagorean Theorem, every explorer who sailed the rough seas
of 3rd-period History, no land where they served lunch in sight.
And later, the name of every bar you learned to spend long nights in,
trying to forget it all, remembering perfectly well
the number of the cab someone always calls for you, how it gets you
miraculously home.

                    So is it asking too much of our abductees to know
by heart that beam of blue, immobilizing light that floated them on board?

The silvery suits and avocado heads of the alien crew?
The lasers and precision instruments that opened some private part of them
and for once it didn't hurt like they knew it would? The star-map
on the wall, with the usual red arrow: *Don't You Wish You Were Here?*
The number of light-years until the next rest stop and maybe at least
where they left the car, even if the goddamn keys they can't find
are lost by now in some deep pocket of space too unlikely to remember?

When we were young we never would have dreamed
of admitting that we hadn't seen anything yet. We were going around
in circles, all our precarious featherweight cargo stuffed into
the rusted-out Chevy of our lives. With a speaker still
hooked on the window so we wouldn't feel as alone: *Not of This Earth.*
The Man from Planet X. We couldn't help humming
right along through the static with the soundtrack's every flutter
and wow. We were never too far from the Starlight.

The way these people tell it, we may never know what we're missing
until it's almost too late. They've been ruined or redeemed, depending
on which version needs believing most. That such a thing's actually
possible, either way, should be enough: that today anyone understands
in any case a little more than yesterday how some of us ended up
astonishingly here, dressed in these strange clothes, dazed
but remarkably ready to go, one more mysterious incision we can point to
in an arm, in a leg, in the thin skin of days
that more or less holds us together. Where something's been added
or taken away, if only we could go back over our arithmetic.

We weren't always quite this suggestible, taking whatever instructions
we think we can live with: when we wake up, we will remember nothing.
Or far too much. So often what comes back is sized to fit
no matter what we believe we've lost out on: a few minutes, a day,
a leap year, a lifetime. And sometimes we're so anxious to make that up,
we do. By now you've got to know the feeling.

You're barely aware of turning the key in the ignition, and out of nowhere
it's you, emerging from the car way too many miles later
with no real idea where you were when the scenery changed. You might think
on the one hand *I'm lucky to be alive,* but on the other, *every day
is like this.* Even though both hands on the wheel were yours, steering
with an uncanny sense of direction.

                              We're all making it up
as we go along: how fast is too fast. When we noticed the sky
clouding over. What we should have said to the attendant at the Starlight
shining his flashlight into our back seat, looking for the same thing
we're still looking for today: a certain dark secret more-of-us than ever
we can probably afford to own up to.
And some of us are not about to be stopped if we can help it, not
this time, now that we're finally getting somewhere. Now
that those Starlight nights are behind us, when anything forgettable
couldn't possibly hurt us beyond belief, and those hours we wasted
hoping for once we'd get lucky during *The Day the Earth Stood Still*
meant nothing to us, with all the time in the world.